Like, A Metaphor

poems

Like, A Metaphor

poems

by
Tom Schmidt

Encircle Publications, LLC
Farmington, Maine USA

Like, A Metaphor ©2021 Tom Schmidt

Paperback ISBN-13: 978-1-64599-275-2
Kindle ISBN-13: 978-1-64599-276-9

All rights reserved. No part of this book may be reproduced in any form by any mechanical or electronic means including storage and retrieval systems without express written permission in writing from the publisher. Brief passages may be quoted in review. Rights to individual poems remain with the author.

Editor: Cynthia Brackett-Vincent
Book and book cover design: Eddie Vincent/ENC Graphics Services
Cover Image: Rubén Rodriguez, Unsplash.com

Sign up for Encircle Publications newsletter and specials
http://eepurl.com/cs8taP

Printing: Walch Publishing, Portland, Maine

Mail Orders, Author Inquiries:
Encircle Publications
PO Box 187
Farmington, ME USA 04938
info.@encirclepub.com

Online orders:
encirclepub.com

To Merry, soul companion and meter maid

Contents

These poems emerge from actual encounters—tragic, edifying, unintentionally amusing—with my rural and urban students in California, Oregon, and Vermont. Although they were collected over many years, I arrange them here as stories from a single day—which in one sense they are.

Two Students Before Class, 7:30 & 7:45 1

10 a.m.: The Metaphorical Object Essay

Hector Brings a Little Blue Towel to Class 4
John Brings a Bic Click to Class 5
Molly Brings F-Bombs to Class 6
Margola Brings an Old Necklace to Class 7
Pete Brings a Flashlight to Class 8
Jack Does Not Bring His AR-19 to Class 9
Sara Brings Her Green Eyes and a Douglas Fir Sprig to Class . . 10
Jessie Brings a Bowl of Crumbled Leaves to Class 11
Brad Taps the Bezel of His Rolex in Class 12
Steve Brings a Chisel to Class 13

During Office Hours, She Asks to Close the Door 14

Early Afternoon, I Grade Several Essays

Happy Place 18
Light Years and Stuff 19
Head Shot 20
Vanilla, But Stars 21

If a Parody Falls in a Forest of Gen-Whatevers . . .

We Swipe Screens. 24
Ozymandias for Windows 25
The Whole Truth about Half 26
Do You Grade on Writing? 27

Mid-Afternoon, I Ponder Academia

Scholar Ships 30
The Physicist and the Theologian 31
Asterisk. 32
Late Afternoon, I Leave My Office 33
Years Later, I Go Back to School 34

Credits 36
About the Author. 37

Two Students Before Class, 7:30 & 7:45

Can I talk to you?
    I need to talk to you
This is awkward but
    I'm getting a B- right now
I can't think of anyone else
    In your class
And you seem like someone
    This is unacceptable
Who would listen
    You need to understand
You need to understand
    My goal is to open a chain
I'm married
    Of dress shops
But it's not going well
    I need A's
My wife says she's leaving
    And your class stands
And I don't know what to do
    In my way
She is my whole world
    So what are you
What should I
    Going to do about this?
Do?

10 a.m.: The Metaphorical Object Essay

Assignment: Write four pages about a common object that has significance only to you, consider how it may represent you, then bring it to class to describe.

Hector Brings a Little Blue Towel to Class

Ten hours, six days, he pulled
green from brown soil, life from yellow kernels.
Grandfather's grandfather smelled of it.
No one asked him why,
but my grandmother told me he once laughed
and said he could only close his eyes at night
when he saw no hunger in hers.

After classes I'm at AutoSplash, where cars
line up like stalks of maize,
soap and wax on chrome, spray shine on black tires;
I smell of it.
Eight hours, six days, I rub;
at night I close my eyes on a thousand
towels, but tomorrow I return, laughing.

You ask me why.
I have not seen my grandmother in years, and you
have never seen my daughter.

John Brings a Bic Clic to Class

I'm just going to put this out there, in high school I was popular and everything, I mean, captain of the soccer team and pretty good grades but home kind of sucked, anyway I got this job part time at an appliance store and my boss was so cool, he was like, a mentor for life, like who cares about appliances, right? But he'd take me to lunch and talk about stuff with me, and I don't know, it was just, well it lasted two years, including last summer, and once he gave me this pen, that's the only thing he gave me, I mean a thing I could touch, and I know, it's like, it's just this cheap
Bic Clic,
no big deal, and—

I didn't think I was going to lose it, sorry, shit, I think
I'm in love with him.
Wow, I just said that.
And I'm straight.
Does that make any sense at all?
God, I'm really blowing this, aren't I. Okay, anyway,
here's this pen, and I'm—
I'm going to
keep it.

Molly Brings F-Bombs to Class

Wait, I'm supposed to bring something
meaningful from my room that's, like, a metaphor?

Can I bring a bong?

Oh, fuck. Why does the college care about that?

What if I buy a new one so
it doesn't have any residue on it?

Oh, fuck.

Well, I just don't get this.

Note: It may not be a shock to learn that "Molly" dropped out of college three days later. May you find clear paths, dear, through life's confusion. And thanks for the book title.

Margola Brings an Old Necklace to Class

A blood-red garnet, gilded filigree;
My Nana sent the necklace next-day air,
The day after she died it came to me.

Mere costume stuff, no value I could see,
Bent clasp and broken chain beyond repair,
A blood-red garnet, gilded filigree.

A note from her last nurse supplied the key
To open up the keepsake's when and where;
The day after she died it came to me.

It made the journey, inexplicably,
From Lodz to Bergen-Belsen to Bel-air,
A blood-red garnet, gilded filigree.

A common bauble prized uncommonly:
Not gem but journey rendered it so rare—
The day after she died it came to me.

I grasp it now, this broken, worn debris
And know of whom, not what, I am the heir.
A blood-red garnet, gilded filigree;
The day after she died it came to me.

Pete Brings a Flashlight to Class

To kill it, they said at the store,
Shoot it (but I had no gun) or
Dunk the trap in the river,

So after midnight, I tied a rope to the cage,
Tossed it in, and pointed this flashlight to make sure
What would happen happened.

Even through those wires and that dark water
Its eyes aimed at me and glowed
Kind of yellowy gold. After a minute, maybe two,

The gold light was there, then it wasn't.

Just like that. The light went out.
I pulled up the cage, the river gurgled,
I dug a hole and buried the thing.

There is probably an explanation.
About the light, I mean.
I only know it went out, just like that.

Also I know that
Next time I kill something, I will be
Humane about it. I will look away.

Jack Does Not Bring His AR-19 to Class

Okay then I'll just give you my notes
For my speech

How to Clean an AR-19

(If teacher won't allow in class, draw on board)
To clean:
Remove magazine
Then receiver cover, coil, spring assembly
Lubricate barrel, gas tube, action
Reassemble
Explain about auto, semi-auto options
(Remember eye contact!)
What it means to me, 4 f's family freedom fun faith
Answer objections:
Mass killings by crazy people, not responsible
2nd amend, govt always starts little grabs more
Self-defense, Chinese may invade, militia against feds
Conclusion (eye contact!):
<u>Memorize</u> founding fathers quotes
Also Clint Eastwood, Ted Nugent
Questions?

Sara Brings Her Green Eyes and a Douglas Fir Sprig to Class

After she left, his folks raised me.
He was out with the crew six days a week,
Clear-cutting, mostly.
I hate that, the ridge looks like a bad haircut, I said,
When I was nine, about a week before
A Doug fir rolled over him, he laughed and said
Yup, and they grow back just like hair too.

He slept late Sundays, took me places,
Before sleep knelt next to my bed,
Crooned a slow version of "Brown Eyed Girl,"
Oh Daddy my eyes are green, I said but
He said it's about the You and the My
Which I get now,
And it's all I've got of him since that one time

He wasn't looking, just that one time.
The crew broke up and went who knows where,
His folks took over but they got in a car wreck so
Now it's just me to remember
     If I do.
It was a mistake floating his ashes like they did,
Now the river's got him, and it's gone,
That particular water, I mean.

When I was nine, just before the log,
And I said that about clear cutting and
He said that about hair, I should have said
No, with trees it's different.
The ones that grow back aren't the same trees,
And pretty soon nobody's left
To remember the ones cut down.

Jessie Brings a Bowl of Crumbled Leaves to Class

Fall:
to understand do not go outside, do not read Keats,
read my sister Annie's body, leaf-like it rustles,
crackles there under heavy sheets, almost
gone gray eyes staring from behind
mummy strips of soiled bed things, beneath
only bones, bones
where once that lovely
curve swept smooth from hip to rib
cage, cage now where something
nearly not Annie bare beats the bars,
rattles just a little, leaf before the last wind,
patter of sleet against the window pane.
Do not go outside, ever,
to understand:
fall.

Brad Taps the Bezel of His Rolex in Class

Grandpa is rich, he got me this
Watch, last summer last
Time I saw him he wasn't quite but looked pretty much
Dead, white hair skin lips sheets walls nurse dress,
Lids low, looking hard at
Nothing I could see, jaw slack slow scraping the last
Bits of air over
Time.
Once he said it's
Time you took some of my
Money, son, get you into a good
School get you a decent
Job, then paused for a
Time and said, Get you enough
Money to afford the
Time to find what
Money can't buy, but
What that was
He didn't say, and I'm here two thousand miles
Away and yesterday they said, Come
Now, there isn't much
Time.

Steve Brings a Chisel to Class

What does justice look like?
My dying artist uncle asked, and I said,
That's easy, a bronze statue of a woman
in robes, blindfolded,
holding up scales. Precisely,
he said, you can almost hear
the correct little clicks of those
weights in the balance. Now,
he said, What does mercy look like?
That one stumped me.

Is there a lesson here, I asked, and
he said, Perhaps sculpt a woman
in a bathrobe, making a ham sandwich,
and her scowling boy, who prefers
peanut butter. Or carve
Bienvenu foisting his candlesticks
on cringing Jean Valjean.
Or fashion a brittle father
rushing down the clay path
to embrace his prodigal, but—

I get the idea, I said,
There would have to be two.
Not quite, he said.
There would also have to be
movement. Not easy with statues,
with things that stay put, things done
so right that they make little clicks.

During Office Hours, She Asks to Close the Door

Please, this is really personal and
other students keep walking by.

Oh, I see.

Well then, here goes.
I'm pregnant. The father is not
involved, and he won't be.
I have a clinic appointment for
tomorrow—you know what I'm saying?
but I want to talk
to you first. I thought—

I'm so sorry, I didn't think
I was going to cry. You're sure
we can't close the door?

Okay, I'll be okay. But here's
the thing. If I keep it, I'll have to
drop out, plus I come from a really
religious family, and they are
going to be
devastated if—

Yeah, I know... I guess.

Three months.

A month ago.

Pretty much night and day, but no,
nobody else knows. I mean, you teach
ethics and stuff, and I thought—

I did, about something else.
They're okay,
I mean, she was okay, but
I felt like, I don't know,
somebody's professional
problem
to solve.

See? That's what I mean. It's like you're
messed up like me, but I think a little
wiser? Like a mirror, and I'm one too, but
mine is all foggy right now.
Yeah, okay.

Uh-huh.

Uh-huh.

Really? That means
so much right now.

I'm a wreck, I know.

Okay, I will, either way. You would do
that? Really?

I will. I will. Thank you so much.

I'll look... No, nobody
waiting. Should I close it now
on my way out?

Note: The young woman whose half of the conversation I recall in this poem chose to drop out of college and move back home. I heard from her once more, three years later, when she described the happy toddler that she had precariously, profoundly chosen.

Early Afternoon, I Grade Several Essays

Assignment: take the full hour to compose an essay in class responding to a prompt chosen by the professor.

Happy Place

So to be a nurse's aid
you have to take this dumb course
where they make you write an essay in an hour

and the directions say, "Describe a simple pleasure
that figures highly in your life"

and the teacher smiles like he's doing us a favor and says
"Find your happy place, but you are not allowed
to fly around the room."

Ha ha. What he don't know.

Like, in life you don't write essays.
And in life, happy places are way off somewhere
when you were a kid
or if you're Wendy hoping for Neverland, off somewhere
in the sky.
But me, I gotta go off and clock in at the BiMart right after class
and anyway it's hard to write with the hand he smashed
with a bottle last night after he staggered in from his
happy place.

Light Years and Stuff

"What makes me wonder" most is distances.
Here I launch into astrophysics, but
Before I bring up billions and trillions
Of galaxies and light years and stuff,
Let me just admit my ignorance
At the beginning, because it's the beginning
That caught me, when they explained
About the new orbiting telescope soon to
Replace the Hubble, which will take
Pictures so far into deep space that—
Because it takes so long for the light
To get here from there, and the universe
Is thirteen billion years old—the images
Will represent what happened then.
That's right, we will soon have a snapshot
Of the beginning, although to what end
I'm not sure. I would rather point the thing
The other way and see how it all ends,
But there you go, I don't get astrophysics.
Out near the edge of a middling galaxy,
A smallish star warms my face
And dances on the surface of a tear
From ninety million miles away, while
I fail to comprehend the three thousand miles
That separate me from California,
Or the distance—if that's what it is—
Between me and my daughter who lives there,
Much less the billions and trillions of miles
That divide me from you when I try to say
I'm afraid of the dark, of all that space.

Head Shot

My sergeant said take him out and you don't think
plus the guy was running at us low plus I was scared
so I raised my arms there was a pop and he was down
half his head including where the eyes were just gone
and then what was left in that bone bowl kind of slid
halfway out into a puddle and mixed with the rain,
yeah, sometimes it rains and gets cold in Kandahar.

So here I am taking classes in American rain and cold
and this shrink they send me to says the right stuff
about how I did what I had to even though they
never found any weapons on the guy, like what the
fuck was he running at us for, and in the dreams
he keeps running without the top half of his head
right up to me grinning like he knows something
I don't, I mean where's it at, that part of my head?

Note: This fragile young man, who shook constantly from PTSD, asked my permission (Sir!) to calm himself by chewing tobacco in class with the promise that he would spit discreetly into a Diet Coke bottle. On one condition, son, that you try to forgive me and anyone else who owes you infinitely more than a glib "thank you for your service."

Vanilla, but Stars

You said to write something that people might not believe,
So here goes, but first you need to know some other stuff,
Like my husband John works hauling gravel for Copeland,
Our girl Emily is eleven, she's into Taylor Swift and texting,
And our Jason is six, he's into monster trucks and dinosaurs,
We rent a little house here in town where we both grew up.
I'm hoping to get my associate's degree, I'm not sure for what
But John says I'm the smart one, and anyway, all this so far
Is about as vanilla as it gets, but that's the point, how it started.

Me and John were up in the Siskiyous right after his discharge
Camping on a summer night way up on top of Bolan Mountain.
It was about two in the morning, we were looking up at the sky
When this huge shooting star came down right in front of us
In slow motion, like it was going to land down in Bolan Lake,
And just seconds later a second shooting star, also in slow motion,
But then, when our eyes followed the second star down, we saw
In a clearing twenty feet away two deer, a buck and a doe
With their heads up, I swear, they were staring at those stars too.

We sat there and didn't say anything for maybe ten minutes,
The deer slowly walked away, and John turned to me and said
Will you marry me, and I said yes, and that's pretty much it.
We didn't tell anybody at first, we wanted it to be our secret.
Later when we told a few, we could tell they didn't believe us,
And hey, if we weren't both there we probably wouldn't either.
So we keep it now like a little treasure in a box. We have that
When John gets his hours cut back, when the kids have the flu,
When it rains, when it's all just vanilla. We still have the stars.

If a Parody Falls in a Forest of Gen-Whatevers . . .

We Swipe Screens
after "We Real Cool" by Gwendolyn Brooks

THE UPLOADERS TO iCLOUD.
SEVEN AT THE STARBUCKS.

We swipe screens. We
Stream scenes. We

Remote. We
Don't vote. We

Plug our ears, we
Mp3ers. We

Text, we tweet. We
Friend, don't meet. We

Defer prices we
Pay for devices.

Ozymandias for Windows

    after "Ozymandias" by Percy Bysshe Shelley

I got an email from somebody's friend
Which said—"Please forward this to one and all";
I picked an address group and then hit Send.
It was an image, jpeg, I recall,
That trembled, beckoned me to comprehend
For fractions of a second as I gazed;
But having little time for what things mean,
I clicked it into cyberspace unfazed;
Let others heed its import if they may:
"My name is Bill, I've conquered all I've seen:
Look on my Works, and do not count the cost!"
That was all. And on went my full day
    Of multi-tasking with the faceless lost
    Who send me messages from far away.

The Whole Truth about Half

A day or two before one school year's end,
From underneath my corner desk I slid
My cardboard box of pedagogue's supplies:
A host of Post-its, staples, markers, pens,
And in addition, much to my dismay,
A pair of hairy thighs with one bare tail—
The nether end of Rattus norvegicus—
Intact and dry, no mark of knife or teeth,
No blood, no nest, no droppings, not a clue
Accounting for its provenance or presence.
I called in reinforcements: PhDs
In history, biology, and math,
The brain trust of our preppy little world.
This fourfold Sherlock surely would rule out
Impossibilities and leave the truth.
Our minds gnawed through the few alternatives:
A carnivore or cannibal of rats
Begins with ends (no rodent left behind),
But here are only haunches, nothing else,
No bones, no turds—absurd! the group concurred.
And yet, no student craving fame would stash
A desiccated rodent in a box
Where, undetected, it might lie for months;
Moreover, whither went the headed half?
A more expressive trophy, to be sure,
Yet not a trace had graced another class.
So round and round we chased our clever tales,
Scenarios successively ruled out,
Which left me, as the literary one,
No solace but of poetry, alas:
That once, for me, someone gave a rat's ass.

Do You Grade on Writing?

Its me. I would of come to class to-day,
But both my kids are still to sick and there
Dad works, plus grammer (husbands mom) wont stay
More then two hours, which I dont think is fair,
Shes in our single wide out back so why
She cant help me some more I just dont get,
Ok, your probly thinking tmi :)
My questions on the homework, I forget
On Tuseday did you say we could or not
Use I on essays? I wrote all I can,
A half a page but that's asfars I got,
And do you grade on writing? Yours, Sue Ann
   P.S. If I missed anything today
   Just send it in an email back ok?

Mid-Afternoon, I Ponder Academia

Scholar Ships

Grand tenure-blown flotilla, here we sail
In ties, in tweeds, into this busy harbor
Where we unload or load our fishy cargo;
We're moderately sure of relatively
True abstractions, absolutely sure
Of falsity in our opponents' claims.
Well, it's a job—and this its smelly port;
The whores, the bars, the fights but metaphors,
Reality the glazed eyes of our charges
Who stare at distant shores, but not at us.

The Physicist and the Theologian

Today a black hole swallowed Stephen Hawking.
By quark of fate or faith, infinity
Ago, I stood a Cambridge student gawking
As he rolled past me into Trinity.
Eternal verities awaited me
Across St. John's Street where my grad advisor
Dispensed divine research advice, whilst he,
The famous physicist, a quantum wiser,
Nudged joystick left, chose Newton over Knox;
What cosmic irony for us to place
His ashes in a dark Westminster box
Instead of shooting them out into space.
    Both then and now, in time's Brief History,
    I watched him pass into God's mystery.

Asterisk

It happens to be William Stafford today.
I like this poem, "Earth Dweller,"
So I make my little check next to the title in the table of contents
Or an asterisk if it's really good.
Maybe I'll memorize it one day.
My other one hundred and thirty-seven volumes of poetry
Filled with check marks and asterisks will be pleased.

Late Afternoon, I Leave My Office

Between black clouds, late fierce light slants
A threat of storm on grass
That students and scholars do not tread.
No, we respect the paths made for us.

This is the same grass I did not trod
In a Cambridge courtyard
Where Isaac Newton once measured
The speed of sound. I kept to paths.

Now, in the interval between flash and boom,
I calculate that none of us is far
From the apple of gravity that drops
Near enough the path to reach.

Years Later, I Go Back to School

I sneak back to campus, summer Saturday.
Someone has left Porter Hall open.
I stand at the lectern, fill the empty
Rows with freshmen,
Whisper the first words of my opening lecture,
And the room gets smaller,

Like my third grade playground,
Where it seemed miles from the fence
To Miss Tillinger
Who blew her whistle to retrieve us,
All crewcuts and ponytails, Karens and Bills,
Endowed with time to cross vast distances,

Like the hundred yards to my old office, where
I peek through blinds
At the latest occupant's scholarly stacks:
A thousand familiar volumes, thick with knowing,
But almost none, as I recall,
Contain pictures.

No whistle sounds, but I know that
Despite my inconspicuously professorial appearance,
Lingering
Will get me sent to the principal's office for sure,
So I climb the hill to the parking lot—
Not as steep as I remembered—and drive away,
Red-eyed, to the grownups.

Credits

Blue Collar Review: "Familias"
(here titled "Hector Brings a Little Blue Towel to Class")

Christian Century: "Light Years and Stuff," "The Physicist and the Theologian," "Statues" (here titled "Steve Brings a Chisel to Class")

Enough to Drink or Drown (chapbook, Kelsay Books, 2020): "Light Years and Stuff"

Final Exam (anthology, Brooks Street Books, 2020): "Reach" and "Commencement" (here titled "Late Afternoon, I Leave My Office" and "Years Later, I Go Back to School")

Jewish Literary Journal: "Margola the Heir" (here titled "Margola Brings an Old Necklace to Class")

Journal of Classical Poets: "Ozymandias for Windows" and "Email Sonnet" (here titled "Do You Grade on Writing?")

Northern New England Review: "Pest"
(here titled "Pete Brings a Flashlight to Class")

War, Literature, and the Arts: "Head Shot"

About the Author

Tom Schmidt earned a PhD at Cambridge University and taught religion, literature, and writing over a span of four decades in three states, working in several types of institutions and with students across the socio-economic spectrum. Along the way, Tom's writing interests turned from academic to imaginative. In the past ten years, he has published two books exploring the intersection of scholarship and fiction, two magical realist novels, and numerous poems in literary journals. His first poetry chapbook, *Enough to Drink or Drown*, appeared in 2020. Tom retired from teaching in 2015 and lives in Vermont with his wife Merry.

www.ingramcontent.com/pod-product-compliance
Lightning Source LLC
Chambersburg PA
CBHW071255070526
44583CB00017B/2484